Can You Guess Where I Am ?

Written by Andrew A. Williams

Illustrated by ArtDan

CAN YOU GUESS WHERE I AM?

ISBN: 979-8-218-55633-4

To my mom and dad.
Thanks for taking me on amazing adventures!

Mommy, daddy, and I take a plane ride.
Across the ocean, we fly and glide!

Can you guess where I am?

We land real smooth and take a drive to a nearby dive.

Can you guess where I am?

Surf
4

I walk outside and smell salt in the air.
The sun is shining bright and the wind is fair.

Can you guess where I am?

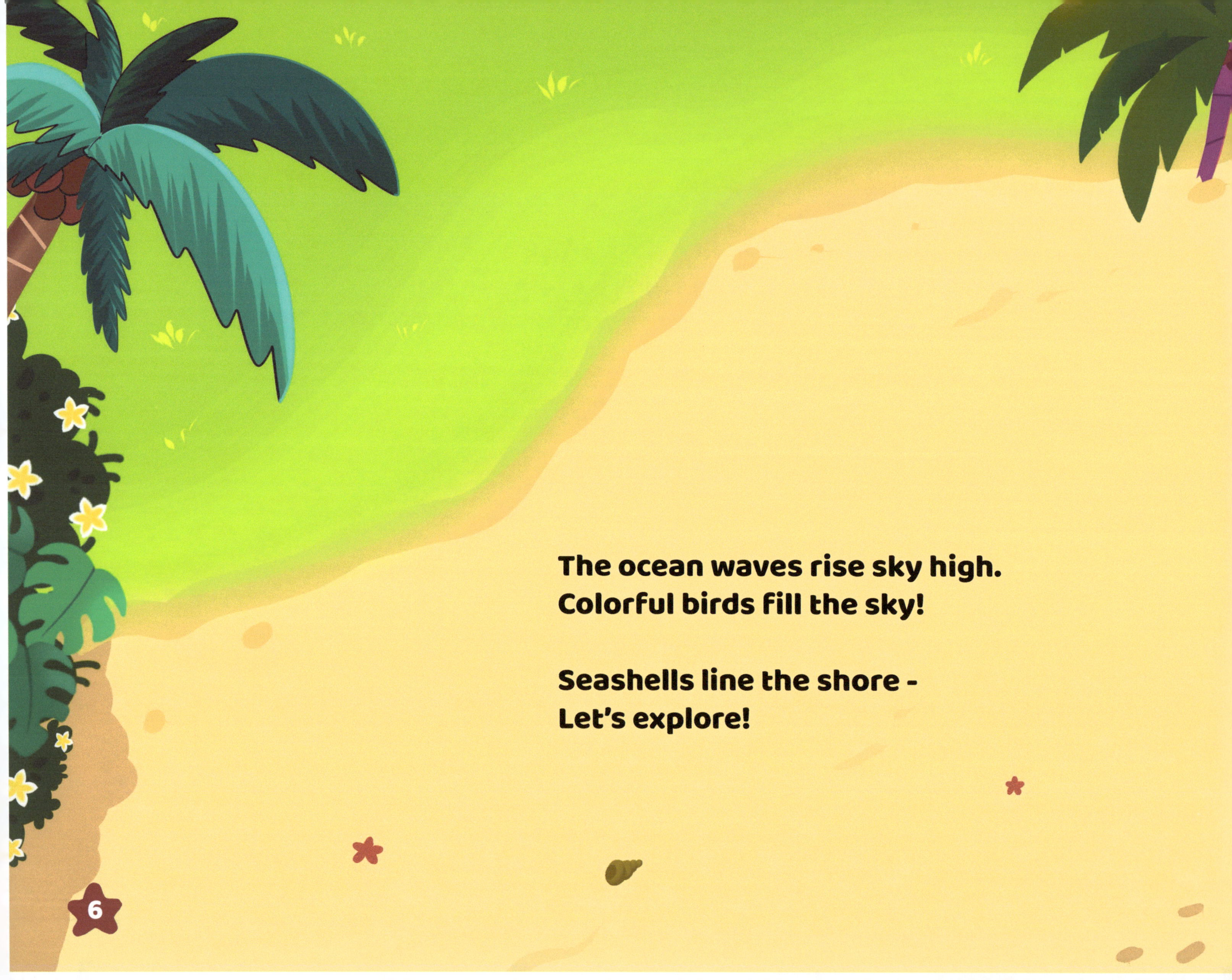

The ocean waves rise sky high.
Colorful birds fill the sky!

Seashells line the shore -
Let's explore!

Green mountains are endless.
Many happy people are all around.
There are many adventures to be found!
8

Mommy makes a lei.
Daddy gets me fruit.
There is so much to
learn and do!

Can you guess where I am?

BEACH
HOTEL
MARKET

9

I play on a beautiful tropical beach
all day long.
A ukulele rings out a lovely song.

A colorful rainbow I see.
There's no place I'd rather be
than here with the ones I love.

Where am I?
Of course, Hawaii!
I've been once before
and I'm so excited to go again.
Best of all I got to tell you about it my friend!

I'll see you on my next adventure!
14

DID YOU KNOW?

In this section, you will discover the meanings behind different pictures from this book and what they can teach us about this beautiful culture. We hope you learn something new!

KUKUI NUT LEI

The special necklace Andrew is wearing is called a Kukui Nut Lei. A lei can be made in several ways including flowers and kukui nuts. His lei is black and white. It holds special meaning to the culture and traditions of Hawaii.

REEF TRIGGERFISH

This little fish is called the Reef Triggerfish. It is found mostly in the Western Pacific Ocean. Its scientific name is the Rhinecanthus rectangulus.

UKULELE

This instrument is called a Ukulele. It makes beautiful music. Its melodies have been used to touch people worldwide.

Did you learn something new? We want to hear from you!
Visit us online at www.ajsworldmap.com

SURFING

Surfing is a surface water sport where a person can ride a wave on a special board while standing or lying down.

In the past, the length and type of wood used for the surfboard distinguished who was royalty or not.

I'IWI BIRDS

This special bird is called an I'iwi. The I'iwi are members of the honeycreeper family. They are currently on the Endangered Species List.

RAINBOWS

Beautiful rainbows adorn the skies of the Hawaiian islands. They appear so regularly that Hawaii is often referred to as the Rainbow Capital of the World. (BONUS FACT) Hawaii is the 50th U.S. state and its capital is Honolulu.

YOU'RE INVITED TO JOIN OUR COMMUNITY!

www.ingramcontent.com/pod-product-compliance
Lightning Source LLC
Chambersburg PA
CBHW041037120726

48006CB00006B/1221